D09988265

. . . A wise man's heart
discerneth both time
and judgment.

Ecclesiastes 8:5

Spiritual Timing
Discerning Seasons of Change in the Realm of the Spirit

by
Roberts Liardon

Harrison House
Tulsa, Oklahoma

Unless otherwise indicated, all Scripture quotations are taken from the *King James Version* of the Bible.

Some Scripture quotations are taken from *The Amplified Bible, New Testament*. Copyright © 1954, 1958 by The Lockman Foundation, La Habra, California.

Spiritual Timing —
Discerning Seasons of Change
in the Realm of the Spirit
ISBN 0-89274-850-8

Published by Harrison House, Inc.
P. O. Box 35035
Tulsa, Oklahoma 74153

Contents

 **Roberts Liardon** was born in Tulsa, Oklahoma. He was born again, baptized in the Holy Spirit, and called to the ministry at the age of eight, after being caught up to Heaven by the Lord Jesus.

Roberts was powerfully commissioned by the Lord to study the lives of God's great "generals" — men and women of faith who were mightily used by God in the past — in order to learn why they succeeded and why they failed.

At age fourteen, Roberts began preaching and teaching in various churches — denominational and non-denominational alike — Bible colleges and universities. He has traveled extensively in the United States and Canada, and his missions outreaches have taken him to Africa, Europe, and Asia. Many of his books have been translated into foreign languages.

Roberts preaches and ministers under a powerful anointing of the Holy Spirit. In his sermons, Roberts calls people of all ages to salvation, holiness and life in the Holy Spirit.

Through Roberts' ministry around the world, many people have accepted God's call to yield themselves as vessels for the work of the Kingdom.

1

Time Can Be Your Friend

That he [we] no longer should live the rest of his [our] time in the flesh to the lusts of men, but to the will of God.

1 Peter 4:2

We need to understand as the Body of Christ, that God has a central point from which every arena of our life operates, whether individually or corporately. It's called **"time."**

From the operation of that one word, lives can move forward with God or be hindered; nations can advance spiritually or regress. It all depends upon our understanding and cooperation with the timings of God. One of the greatest needs we seem to have is how to understand and operate with spiritual timings.

As soon as you are born again, the sensitivity to the timings of God should operate in your life. Every moment from that point forward is meant to be lived according to the will of the Father.

The world has made an attempt to harness time. They have created time-management seminars and have tried to teach millions how to save time and be more effective with it. I am not against time management by any means. Some have become so time-consumed, they will even allow their values to deteriorate as long as it saves some time.

Earth time usually means "rush." We have fast food, rush hour traffic, instant this and instant that. People in the natural fight with time. It frustrates them and produces anger. They don't like the pace of it. They either want things to slow down or to speed up. To the world, time is an enemy.

The only place that time becomes your friend is in the Spirit realm. People who live in the Spirit know how to work and walk with time.

God introduced His timing to us in Genesis chapter 1.

Heb.? At. **(In the beginning God created the heaven and the earth.**

Genesis 1:1

That verse, the very first in the Bible, points out God's timing. Everything He did was based on timing. When the universe was created, each part of it was made on a certain day, in a certain time. He formed every part of the galaxy to operate in His timings. First, He created the earth and everything surrounding it. Then, God created all of the plants, fish, animals and birds. Finally, in His perfect timing, He created man. At this point, all of God's creation walked harmoniously with Him.

But in Genesis chapter 3, man's timing began with the Fall. When man fell, he lost his ability to hear and follow God without a special endowment from heaven. He no longer had the ability to operate in God's timing on his own. Generation after generation produced only trial and trouble unless God intervened.

All through the Old Testament days, God gave information to the people concerning Himself, through the prophets. He still provided them with the ability to know Him and serve Him. The understanding of spiritual times, even in those days, came from being committed to God.

One of the things that Jesus came and produced for us at Calvary was the ability to perceive and regain the correct timings of God. By receiving His redemption and walking in the Spirit, we can come back into it. We can fine-tune our spirits to know when to be in the right place at the right time, or to stay out of the right place at the wrong time. Through knowing God and His ways, we can build the character within ourselves, that will position us strategically in the proper season.

When you live in the spirit, time is lovely. Time is a blessing. A Spirit-filled man can walk in step with God and work the works of God without stress or strain. He understands time.

To a Spirit-filled man, time means stability and nurturing. Time matures and heals. It brings understanding and abilities. Time expands and deepens our insight. When we walk with time, we walk with patience. As a result, we have the ability to possess our whole man, physically, emotionally and spiritually.

Walking securely in the timing of God alleviates fear. There is no fear or doubt in the proper timing of God. Godly timing produces courage, boldness, security and strength.

God's clock is always ticking, but it's not like man's clock. If we follow man's clock, by what some men say some of us would be in the millennium by now.

> **Why, seeing times are not hidden from the Almighty, do they that know him not see his days?**
>
> **Job 24:1**

Fear – one of the greatest DISABILITIES Spirit in extreme, petrifies, immobilises, paralizes

Job is the oldest book in the Bible. By reading the statement he made, we can see the wisdom and understanding Job had, even in his day. He lived long before Moses came, and still he knew that those who truly know God know His ways and His timing.

Life in the spirit realm has a timing to it just as life in the natural. If you stay close to the Lord, you will be able to move according to His seasons.

It is important for us to follow the leading in our spirit. We must learn that it's not always right to move into action because it seems like the thing to do. This kind of obedience only comes from seasons of prayer and intercession.

Prayer alerts your spirit to the commands of heaven. It causes your inner man to take precedence over your mind, resulting in the right action at the right time.

If you will walk strongly in the Spirit, you'll be able to move according to God's clock in everything you do. You will know how much time to spend with certain people, when to build relationships, when to speak and when to withhold. You will know when to move out on the plan of God for your church, your community and your nation.

In Mark 14:41, after much prayer, Jesus stood up and told His disciples.

> . . . **take your rest: it is enough, the hour is come** . . .

Jesus knew by the timing of the Spirit that He was ready to fulfill the greatest work to ever be done — the redemption for all mankind at Calvary.

You don't have to miss the correct timings of God in your life. Some people miss the accurate time to enter the ministry. They know they are called, but their time is not yet come because of preparation purposes and they launch out too soon. Many have aborted their entire ministries because they were not equipped to handle the trouble they encountered.

The Bible says **"a wise man's heart discerneth both time and judgment"** (Eccl. 8:5). We must be able, as the Body of Christ, to know when to go and when to stay; when to speak and when to remain silent. It is our goal to hit accurately the timing of God so that heaven can reap the benefit of a full and bountiful harvest. It is the will of God that we not only be sensitive to the leadings of the Holy Spirit, but that we operate effectively in them. Time is designed by God, to be called one of our dearest friends.

God restores things stolen from us— including years.
See Jeremiah. God invented seconds minutes hours days weeks months (28 days /lunar) years (360 days was) Sabbaths - of days + of years (Sabbatical) Jubilees one year
360° derives from 360 days.
God made mathematic, Man discovered it.

2
Discerning
Times and Seasons

And he said also to the people, When ye see a cloud rise out of the west, straightway ye say, There cometh a shower; and so it is.

And when ye see the south wind blow, ye say, There will be heat; and it cometh to pass.

Ye hypocrites, ye can discern the face of the sky and of the earth; but how is it that ye do not discern this time?

Luke 12:54-56

If we did not understand natural times and seasons, we might go out in the dead of winter in tee shirts and shorts — and freeze to death. On the other hand, we might go outside in the tropics during the summer, wearing overcoats and thermal underwear — and have heatstrokes!

Jesus addressed this spiritual principle to his disciples, the ever-present Pharisees, and **an innumerable multitude of people** (v. 1) on this particular day in Galilee.

Notice that He was fervent on His illustration and did not give His listeners any excuse for ignorance, but called them *hypocrites.* That was a very bold statement!

Jesus' implication was that His hearers should have *known* from Scripture (the Old Testament) that they were living in the time of the Messiah. He did not confine His remarks, as He sometimes did, just to His disciples or to a small crowd. This was an innumerable multitude that He chastised.

I believe if Jesus were walking on the earth today, so that all the Church could see Him with natural eyes, He would be saying something similar to many of us. He not only wants, but expects, those who are faithful to discern spiritual times.

We live in a new day, a new spiritual time. When Jesus said, **"let the dead bury their dead"** (Luke 9:60), He meant, "Let the past be the past." You cannot make spiritual progress living in past times and moves of God any more than you can have growth in your natural life while living in the past.

Jesus said to the multitudes that day in Galilee, "How is it that you know all about the natural side of life, but you cannot tell what times you are in on the spiritual side?"

God does not live in the past. It is always *today* with the Lord. He lives in the now. The greatest results you will have in your life or ministry will come when you walk in the spiritual time in which you are living, when you walk in the *present* anointing.

We are to learn from the past, but we are not to live there. We are to live in the present and lock into the future.

Christians must learn to think in the now, or we will not see God's glory as we should, nor be able to move with Him when He moves. Many churches cherish a time in the past so much that they build a memorial in their minds to it and live there. The best way to respect the past is to build on it for the future.

The great men and women of the Church's past would be the first to push us on out today. Those people who laid the path on which we walk would not be happy to think the Church was living on past glories of what God accomplished through them.

Of course, we need to honor past men and women of God. We need to appreciate and learn from what they accomplished for the Kingdom. But we cannot live or move or have our being in what they did, only in God. The past reputation of the Church, no matter how great, is not the Rock on which we are to stand. To receive today's blessing, we must move in what He is doing today.

It is not the season right now to act like we are about to leave the earth. It is the season to reap the harvest. It is the season to hear from heaven so that we can reap the full potential of souls in all the earth. It is the season to declare the works of God in the nations. It is the time for the Church to regain their sensitivity to repentance.

The trumpet has not yet sounded and we are not in a season to put on the wedding gown. We are betrothed, but we are still wearing army clothes. Wearing a wedding gown in a season of war and harvest makes you stand out as an easy target for the enemy. We must set ourselves to hear accurately what the Spirit of the Lord is doing in the earth today.

The subject of "warfare" should not make you nervous. Those who do not understand the season of transition get very touchy about spiritual warfare. They do not understand that a time of transition, a day of visitation from the Lord, always means spiritual warfare. There is always hard work before the harvest.

In Jesus' day, Satan himself came to war against the Messiah. Demons were stirred up everywhere Jesus went. It was a time of transition. He cast them out, taught his disciples to cast them out, and then made deliverance part of the Great Commission (Mark 16:15-18) — His final instructions of war to His "soldiers."

Revival is in progress worldwide. Revival is for the Church, not for sinners. It means "restoration" and you cannot restore something that has never been.

The Body of Christ always needs refreshing and restoration before the great moves of evangelism and harvest. God uses those times to prepare the "soil" in our hearts before He gathers in the lost. We must be sensitive in this time and understand that "revival" is not to be confused with "evangelism."

Local churches are revived, then they go out and evangelize, gathering in the harvest. Evangelism is the offspring of a church whose heart has been revived. The time of preparation for God's move has been going on for several years now.

If you are living in the past while hearing the message for today, the message will not make any sense to you. You will think it is false or confusing, and you will probably want to come against it — just as the Pharisees did in Jesus' day.

They were trying to live in the past glory of Israel. They had built a memorial to Moses and the Law and were looking backward instead of forward to the New Covenant whose time had come.

You can choose to live in any time zone you want to live in as a Christian. You have the choice to live in the past, if you so desire. You have the opportunity to sit by and wait for the coming of the Lord, if you so decide. But to live on the cutting edge, to be full and alive with the Spirit of God, is to be moving with what God is doing in the earth right now — today.

The Pharisees did not hear the message proclaimed in their day. Although they were to lead the people, they did not know the season and timing of God.

However, the demons knew the spiritual time.

In Matthew 8:29, the Apostle relates how Jesus cast a legion of demons out of a "crazy" man. The demons talked to Jesus.

> **And, behold, they cried out, saying, What have we to do with thee, Jesus, thou Son of God? art thou come hither to torment us before the time?**

You see, even demons are aware that God has a time to do certain things. They knew it was not His time for them to be shut up forever in the lake of fire.

Demons who operate in the low, carnal area are not very intelligent. They do not think or reason. However, those workers for Satan who are part of his hierarchy — the principalities, powers and rulers of darkness (Eph. 6:12) — know what is going on with the Kingdom of God.

If the devil, his angels and demons know about time, then certainly the Body of Christ should set themselves to know.

New Testament Transition

The three years that covered the ministry of John the Baptist and Jesus, were a time of major transition, from the Old Covenant to the New. That is why Jesus' first — and only — message in His hometown of Nazareth made a clear statement of the spiritual season they were in.

> . . . as his custom was, he went into the synagogue
> on the sabbath day, and stood up for to read.
>
> **Luke 4:16**

Notice that Jesus was accustomed to going into the synagogue and reading the text for the day. The people knew Him. This was not the first time He had read the scripture. In verse 17, the Book of Isaiah was given to Him to read.

God arranges situations in His timing, if we do not get in His way. This was the very day that God had appointed for Jesus to declare to His family and neighbors Who He was. God had witnessed in the heart of the synagogue leader, to have Him read from the prophetic Book of Isaiah.

Because they had known Jesus all of His life, they got the first chance to hear that the day of visitation was at hand. Many times, when God sends a person out, He sends them first to their family and friends.

So Jesus, sensitive in His spirit, followed God's timing, although He must have known it would make the religious crowd angry. His example is what we must still follow today.

> The Spirit of the Lord is upon me, because he hath
> anointed me to preach the gospel to the poor;
>
> he hath sent me to heal the brokenhearted,
>
> to preach deliverance to the captives,

and recovering of sight to the blind,

to set at liberty them that are bruised,

to preach the acceptable year of the Lord.

Luke 4:18,19

"The acceptable year of the Lord" was an explicit statement of the time it was on God's clock. He went on to speak:

. . . This day is this scripture fulfilled in your ears.

Luke 4:21

Those words were prophetic for the coming Messiah, and the listeners knew it. But they missed their day of visitation because they clung to the past time of God. They had grown to understand the past and were comfortable there.

Jesus tried to tell them, "These things were foretold for a certain day. Now that day has arrived. It is today." But, they would not hear. They could not sense the appointed time and season of God.

John the Baptist was also a proclaimer of the timings of God in that day. He said:

Repent ye: for the kingdom of heaven is at hand.

Matthew 3:2

I indeed baptize you with water unto repentance: but he that cometh after me is mightier than I, whose shoes I am not worthy to bear: he shall baptize you with the Holy Ghost and with fire.

Matthew 3:11

Then the very next day, he saw Jesus and said:

This is he of whom I said, After me cometh a man which is preferred before me: for he was before me.

John 1:30

17

After Jesus was baptized, John knew Him because of the Holy Spirit's descending on Him like a dove. That was the sign God had given him by which to recognize the Son of God. (John 1:31-34.)

John was aware that he had a work to fulfill before Jesus would come. He knew that his ministry was going to be short. He did not try to minister, or even to live, longer than God needed him to. When Jesus showed up, John said, **"He must increase, but I must decrease"** (John 3:30).

John the Baptist did not fight to stay in charge of the hour. He let Jesus take over. We need to have an awareness not only that times and seasons do change, but we need to know when they change and whether it means we are to increase or decrease.

God Changes the Times and Seasons

In Daniel 2:21, the Bible says God **"changeth the times and seasons."** We must become mature enough in the spirit so that when God changes the times and seasons to which we are accustomed, we do not get angry or upset. We must get to the place where we can see the hand of God moving and move with what He is doing, not against it.

We cannot change times and seasons. We cannot even rearrange them. We cannot hold them still, because God raises up and brings down. He is the One Who does that.

When Daniel found himself in captivity in Babylon, He knew it was God's season for pruning rebellion and idolatry off His people through exile and life in a strange land. Yielding to the judgment — as

God told them to do — would have allowed them to use the time of captivity for genuine repentance and changing of their ways. They could have been blessed in Babylon, and many were. (Jer. 29:4-14.)

In the Book of Ecclesiastes, chapter 8, verse 5, we read:

> **Whoso keepeth the commandment shall feel no evil thing: and a wise man's heart discerneth both time and judgment.**

A wise man knows both the timing of God as well as the judgment of God. A foolish person knows neither.

An immature Christian will cherish something beyond its time. A mature spirit will be joyful over the changing because it is according to God's will. A mature Christian knows God never brings us down — no matter how it looks. He always brings those who love and serve Him up to a better place.

Spiritual Hunger

An important characteristic that causes God to take us from one season to another is spiritual hunger.

In Jesus' day, just as in our day, there were many that were caught up in a past time. But on the other hand, there were also many who had a dissatisfaction in their hearts. They knew, because of the sensitivity to the things of God, that it was time for a change.

There was no longer the peace of relying on the letter of the law that there had been. The desire for the Messiah to come had intensified in their hearts. The Pharisees also intensely wanted Messiah to come, but their desire was in their minds. Their "Messiah" fit their own scenario and not God's. So they missed Him.

Today, there is a hunger for the Word. There is a hunger for the fullness of the five-fold offices. Physical hunger is one of the most powerful drives on the earth, because it is directly related to survival of the body. In the same way, spiritual hunger is one of the most powerful instincts in the spirit realm because it is tied to the survival of our spiritual walk.

When people are starving, they will do things that otherwise they would not do. They will eat things that in better times would not be acceptable at all.

The same is true in spiritual hunger. People are hungry for the written Word and for a direct, personal word from God. They are so hungry to see God move and the prophetic, that in many places, if they are not fed, they try to fill their hunger through false prophecies and false prophets. Some are trying to do it themselves, trying to take hold of the prophetic anointing and they are making big mistakes.

A hunger for anything spiritual is a sign that God's time has changed. God's answer to the spiritual craving in the earth today is on its way. The truth *is* coming in stability and accuracy.

As we continue to prepare our hearts, God will continue to mature His leaders and proclaimers. By staying in the Word of God and prayer, we will continue to sharpen our sensitivity so that we can excel into maturity.

The changing of times and seasons is exciting to those who are hungry for the Spirit of God.

3

A Time for Gifts, Revelation and Offices

A man hath joy by the answer of his mouth: and a word spoken in due season, how good it is!

Proverbs 15:23

In this time of spiritual transition, the Church should be seeking God to find His timing. The believers, and particularly those who minister in the name of the Lord, should find out the times and seasons, for there are certain times that certain things are to be spoken.

A word spoken out of season brings more confusion than blessing. But a word spoken in season brings joy and clarity.

In Isaiah 50:4, the prophet said:

The Lord God hath given me the tongue of the learned, that I should know how to speak a word in season to him that is weary.

We have the ability, by our spirits, to speak the correct words, at the correct time. By speaking the right words at the right time, it will refresh, rearrange, and encourage those who hear. That is our purpose.

You see, the right timing of God will produce an atmosphere in which we can release the revelation inside of us. But if we speak out in the wrong timing, our words produce a counter-reaction in the hearts and minds of the people.

21

When a revelation is spoken and delivered at the right time, it spreads like wildfire and goes everywhere. Many people speaking true words from God have gone through unnecessary persecution because the person delivering the message didn't understand the timing to it. Even a true word, given at the wrong time, can do much damage.

One thing that believers, and in particular, those in the ministry, must learn, is how to know when a word is "in season." So many just hear something and "run with it," causing a negative reaction everywhere they go. Those people need an understanding of time. Just because we have a "word" doesn't mean it is to be delivered at that moment.

Many believers and ministries live in frustration because they try to analyze the timing of God through public opinion, intellect or organization. As a result, they wear themselves out physically, emotionally and spiritually. The ministry suddenly becomes a dreaded chore, followed by disillusionment and sin. Some have even left the ministry, exhausted and seared.

We need to know when to move and when to rest. Faith is now; but results are birthed from accurate timing.

The sign of a mature Christian is his ability to walk accurately in God's timing. A young Christian is characterized by his mistakes with timing. That does not mean he is in deep trouble. It simply means he is in a learning process.

I remember when I was learning this. I would get a message in my heart and hold it. It was so much inside of me that I would stand in front of my mirror and speak it out to myself!

That is hard. You have this strong message inside of you, and it is alive, almost like a baby. It is "kicking" and moving, and you want it to come forth and be born. You begin to say, "When is it going to be time?" If you are not careful, the message can become an irritation to you instead of a blessing.

But when that message came out in God's timing, it was wonderful! It went all over the country when I preached it, because I hit the right time with it. Revelation must be released in accuracy of time. Everything the Holy Spirit gives you belongs in a sequence of His timing.

Unction or Emotion?

I've had prophecies for individuals that I wanted to give them right then. My soul said they needed to hear it, but in my spirit, I had no release to give it. So I had to wait.

We must learn the difference between emotion and unction. You do not give a word from God without the unction. An attempt to move in the Spirit by emotion will pull you out from the correct timing of God every time. Learning and operating with the unction in our spirit will keep us in step with timing. We must speak out of the unction of spirit, not the pull of emotion.

The Greek word "charisma" means "an unguent or smearing"[1] with oil or a salve, and it is usually translated as some form of the word "anoint." The scholars who translated the *King James Version* of the

---

[1]*Strong's Exhaustive Concordance of the Bible*, "unction," reference #5545.

Bible used "unction" only as an English translation of "charisma" one time in the entire Bible. That is in 1 John 2:20:

But ye have an unction from the Holy One, and ye know all things.

Unction simply means "anointing." Do not give a prophecy to anyone unless you have the anointing from the Holy Spirit to do so. There must be a divine stirring inside of you. It is not emotion; it is not rejoicing.

It is not a "good idea" because it would make the person feel better. That unction from God literally draws it out of you, for it is the unction, or anointing, that brings it forth in power.

Sometimes I have a prophecy in my spirit, and I walk into a meeting where the people seem to be really rejoicing, praising God, and ready to receive. But there is no unction on me to give forth the word. Then I go into another meeting where it did not look as if anything was happening. And, boom! There comes the prophecy.

I used to wonder why God would give it to those people and not the ones at the earlier meeting. Then I began to see that only God knows the heart and level of maturity. His prophecies are meant to begin a work immediately when they are received.

During this time of prophetic transition, we must be very sensitive to this fact, especially someone in the five-fold office of the Prophet. If he is not aware of the timing of God, he can get involved in self-inflicted, or self-caused persecution by releasing and doing things without an anointing or before the time. Prophets are very aware of what God is doing today and in the future. Just because they have the ability to "see" what

God will do, doesn't mean it is time to announce it or to try to bring it into manifestation. It is of the utmost importance that Prophets remain sensitive to the timings of God.

Not long ago, I became so tired of hearing "dead" prophecies! I thought if I heard another one, I would scream. "Dead" prophecies are exhortations out of someone's soul. They may even be heartfelt, but they are not prophecies and should not be given forth as such.

No matter how good they sound or how scriptural they are, there is no anointing to prophesy on those words. If people are learning how to operate in the gifts or in the prophetic office, that is one thing. But there are people who have been giving out "dead" prophecies for years.

The unction gives you power to speak out the word of God in a high-ranking force. It carries weight and rearranges the thoughts and the direction we are walking. Our emotions say that an exhortational prophecy means "pat me." But Biblical exhortation means to urge, admonish, push on, warn.

The Apostle Peter wrote that, in old times, men of God spoke by the Holy Spirit not by the will of men. (2 Pet. 1:21.) The New Testament times or present-day times are no different. When a word is spoken in the correct timing with unction, it will come with weight, power and force. The Holy Spirit knows the perfect time.

We must learn not to give forth a word because an auditorium is full or the conditions seem right. It would be easy to release a word from the Lord when excitement is high. But we must train ourselves from the unction within us, not by the excitement level around us. The unction within will direct us into the appointed time.

Time for Prophetic Anointing

One of the main reasons we must be sensitive to the timings of God is because there is coming the heart and thrust of evangelism with a prophetic anointing. To me, the greatest evangelists I have ever seen are the ones with the prophetic anointing. They are prophetic evangelists. They understand the times and seasons of God and they also understand the workings of the prophetic office.

In fact, it is like two streams that are converging together from different directions to form a mighty river. The prophetic stream and the evangelistic stream are meeting head on and will merge. They will not be in conflict.

In the latter part of 1989, the Spirit of God began to bring out of me in prayer a call for the prophetic evangelist to come into the earth, to go through the nations, reaping a harvest by saying and doing things as God directs.

I began to see the prophetic anointing come on some evangelists. But some that I saw it come upon tended to be afraid because they were moved to step out in arenas they were not used to. Some things you learn simply by moving out in faith. However, the natural side of man always wants to understand what is happening before stepping out.

But one particular evangelist I saw moved out with the prophetic anointing, and the manifestation of God was so strong it is hard to describe.

This evangelist was sensitive to changing and timing of the Spirit, and he began to preach on the glory of God. As he began, what he preached started to manifest in the room. I believe that is characteristic of the accurate timing with prophetic anointing. What is preached or taught will come into the room as the ministry gift steps out in faith.

As this evangelist preached, I was sitting on the front row, and I could feel the glory of God come in behind me. The stronger he preached, the stronger the glory became.

His preaching was like prophesying the whole time, without saying, "Thus saith the Lord" in the middle of his sermon. He began this way: "The word of the Lord is . . ." Then the rest of the sermon was the word of the Lord.

Soon, people all over the room began to weep. All of a sudden, they began to come down the aisles without an altar call. Some of them ran to the altar. The glory of God and the conviction of the Spirit was so strong that even those already saved wanted to be saved again! It was one of the most anointed meetings I had ever been in.

All of the five-fold offices are coming into a new day, and a prophetic anointing is going to rest on all of them to a certain degree. There will be prophetic pastors, prophetic teachers, and prophetic evangelists. They are going to operate differently than we are accustomed to seeing.

There have been prophetic evangelists before, because God's "new thing" usually is a restoration of something that has been lost or forgotten by the Church. John the Baptist was one who preached under a prophetic anointing, telling of things to come and warning of judgment at the same time he called the people to repentance. The anointing was what brought conviction. Otherwise, John the Baptist was no different than other "wild men" of his day, who spent solitary time in the desert and came out preaching.

His sensitivity to time, the presence of the Holy Spirit and the prophetic anointing, is what made him different.

Timing With Praise and Worship

There is even coming a prophetic anointing on praise and worship. Tradition is very strong in that area. Many Charismatic or Word of Faith churches got delivered from the hymn book, but then became stuck on transparencies. Some are still at the mercy of the machine that throws lyrics on the wall, or to a certain systematic song order.

It was not the old songs that were the problem. "Religion" had crept in through routinely singing the same old way in the flesh. The newness of the songs fooled us. Because they were fresh, we could really get involved singing them.

But new songs are no substitute for the Holy Spirit anointing, nor are they a sure sign of it. New songs or old songs, it is the spirit we sing them out of that counts.

Some churches have set their entire congregation backwards because of the songs they sang before the message. The ministers leave frustrated because they can't understand why the people couldn't grasp what they delivered to them. The song service left the people stagnant and crusty, making it difficult to receive the full impact of the message.

We need to quit holding on to something because we are comfortable with it and move out with the timing of the Spirit.

Sometimes, just an obedience in action will change the flow.

I was scheduled to speak at a certain church on Mother's Day. Usually, I have a word or a stirring in my spirit, but I could not get anything for the service. Before I left for the church, I looked up scriptures about mothers, and none of them were anointed to me.

I walked into the pastor's office and said, "Pastor, I don't have anything for mothers today."

He said, "That's good, because I preached about that last week."

I thought, "Hallelujah! I don't have to worry about that." But then the real problem came — I did not know what to preach.

So I said, "I'll just go by faith."

The music started and they were singing the usual Charismatic/Word-Faith songs. I was being nice and preferring my brethren, being very sweet and respectful.

Then the Lord said to me, "I want you to dance."

So I began dancing very easily, when the Lord said, "No, no, no!"

I said, "Well, what do You want then?"

He said, "I want the old combined with the new."

I said, "Oh. You mean, don't 'wiggle' but DANCE."

And He said, "Yes."

Now I am coming out of tradition as fast as I can, but there is a little bit left. I am looser than some people, but there are still things I am dealing with.

I said, "But, Lord, it's Mother's Day! Everyone is wearing flowers." I knew God was going to do a work in that place, but I also knew that everyone was dressed up with flowers and with visitors there, no one wanted to sweat — it was Mother's Day!

You see, when the Lord says "dance" to me, that does not mean your normal two-step. That means DANCE. When I dance, I get into it all over. I am everywhere.

Well, I started to dance.

On the way up into the spirit realm, you have to fight demons, whether it is through prayer or praise and worship. Half of the front row went with me.

A member of my staff also moved with me. As soon as I began to really dance, I was in a fight. It was not one of those bringing-down-the-glory dances; it was a we-are-going-to-win dance. There was a controlling spirit dominating that church and God wanted them free.

Sometimes we get into places that we know very little about. We must know the accurate timings of God in order to move correctly with what the Spirit of God intends to do.

We were singing a praise song, full of zeal. The atmosphere was being hit by the praises of the people, when suddenly the musicians started to change over to a worship song.

It was not the time to move from a praise song into a quiet, worship song.

The unction was strong in me, and I said, "Don't do it! Go back to that other song and let's sing."

We went back to the first song, and people all over the building began to enter in with us. But the musicians were not entering into the moving of the Spirit. Because they hadn't been sensitive to the timing of God, they remained startled that the systematic order was changed. They kept trying to be nice and sweet. The Holy Spirit wanted to move among the people, but the musicians were hindering Him.

I finally moved over and stood right in the middle of the instrumentalists. They looked petrified, but I kept saying, "Play with force! Play with force!" Finally, they hit it with force.

Because the musicians had not prepared themselves to be sensitive, we didn't go as far into the realm that God had intended, but it became enough to win. That controlling spirit came down that day, and that was the way it was brought down. For two and a half hours, we sang, danced and sweat.

The service was noisy, yet decent and in order. What most people call "decently and in order" means organizing the Holy Spirit out.

Freedom to that church did not come by preaching or prophesying. It came by being sensitive to God's chosen way of the hour. It came to them by the minstrel and by the dance.

We must be careful not to learn from a "system." We must learn from the unction, or we become religious.

God wants us to move under His unction, not by performance, nor by "working things up" through emotion and the flesh.

Every time I dance and wave my arms under the anointing, the nations are inside of me. When I scream and yell, it is not for those around me, but for the nations.

Dancing without the Spirit is wasted effort and is flesh, but there is an anointing for certain actions and operations. It comes by knowing the accurate timing.

Some musicians and song leaders are not receiving this message because they sing and play out of their heads, not out of the Spirit. Many of their gifts are being aborted because they choose to operate completely in the flesh through intellect and organization. It is so sad to see a prophetic worship leader in bondage to a system.

I do not know music, but I do know how to lead praise and worship in the Spirit. At times there is an anointing, an unction that comes on me for those things. I must hear the timing of God in each service that I minister in. We must learn to operate from that unction, for it will lead to godly results every time.

4

Pitfalls of the Wrong Timing

King David was a man after God's own heart, yet he is a classic example of a leader of God's people who missed the spiritual timing of the hour.

In 2 Samuel 11, there is recorded a tragic incident in David's life. In past years, when I preached on that chapter, I used it as a text for a message on sexual misconduct. However, on an airplane flying home from Europe, the Lord prompted me to reread this story. Then he asked me a question.

He said, "Why did David commit the sins that he did in this instance?"

I began to talk to the Lord about it, and I answered Him with my usual thought on David's situation with Bathsheba.

He said, "Read it again."

> And it came to pass, after the year was expired, *Pesach*
> at the time when kings go forth to battle, that David *New year*
> sent Joab, and his servants with him, and all Israel;
> and they destroyed the children of Ammon, and
> beseiged Rabbah. But David tarried still at Jerusalem.
>
> **2 Samuel 11:1**

The Lord asked me, "What time was it?" *March/April*

I said, "Well, it was the end of the year." *and beginning*

The Lord said, "That is not the time I am talking about. That is natural time. The next sentence tells you

33

the time David should have been in. What time was it otherwise?"

I said, "That verse says it was **at the time when kings go forth to battle.**" Winter is over, Spring has

That was it! David missed the timing that God ordained for him to follow. The sins that he is so remembered for are only the surface of a core problem — he missed the timing.

Where was David at a time when the kings went forth into battle? Where was the king when his men were out fighting for the country and taking territory that the Lord had promised? God gave land to them, but they had to occupy it. Instead of leading the fight for the Lord, David sent his men to fight, while he stayed home.

When people do not move with God's timing for them, they are vulnerable to the traps and temptations of the enemy. David ended up in this story as an adulterer and a murderer, because he did not go with the right time.

Missing God's timing is almost as dangerous as deliberately being disobedient. What it means is that God walks on, and you are not under the shelter of His wings to one degree or another. I believe the degree is associated with how much we are aware of His timings. He will never leave us, but we quite often walk away from Him. He is still our Father, yet we are not in the close fellowship necessary to be in tune with Him. When we are not in tune, or sensitive to the Holy Spirit, we do not hear Him as clearly when He warns us of things to come.

Hosea 4:6 speaks of God's people being destroyed through lack of knowledge. David's lack of insight that to miss God's timing might destroy him almost did exactly that.

Some may say, "But his main problem was not being in enough prayer or communion with God."

Even prayer and studying the Word is not an adequate substitute for obedience, for moving out in God's direction and His time. What prayer and reading the Word will do, however, is to make it more likely that you will hear from God if you are out of His place or time and enable you to get back in tune with the Lord.

Why did David miss the timing of God? He was a strong leader, anointed and chosen by God. As I went on to study this chapter, I saw some important character-building keys that David had neglected at this particular point in his life.

Pride

The main root of David's problem at this time was **pride.** Any leader that is in true, humble authority will be with his people and not on a man-made pedestal.

David placed himself on a pedestal by refusing to be in the battle with his people. After all, he was the king and he could do whatever he wanted, with whom he wanted, whenever he wanted. He could invent his own rules and regulations if he desired. He had the money, the power, the comfort, the reputation and the respect. The people already knew he was a great warrior. He no longer felt he had to maintain it, if he did not feel like it. His reputation was firmly established.

Although these blessings were given to him by God, David chose at this particular time to set himself up as his own law. He chose to remain in the king's palace where it was nice, and easy, and safe.

Walking out from the spiritual timing of God is deadlier than any natural weapon on the battleground.

The evidence of pride has many faces. A haughty attitude is only one sign of it. Another is immorality and uncontrolled desire.

The main reason we would knowingly walk out from the correct timing of God is to get our own way. When we do not walk in the spirit and our heart is not submitted to the will of God, the only thing left to lead us is desire.

> **And it came to pass in an eveningtide, that David arose from off his bed, and walked upon the roof of the king's house: and from the roof he saw a woman washing herself; and the woman was very beautiful to look upon.**
>
> **2 Samuel 11:2**

When we are not sensitive to the timing of God, peace leaves and restlessness comes.

David's mind was obviously racing with thoughts. Driven from sleep with his active mind, he got up, walked out on the roof into the night, and caught a glimpse of a beautiful woman bathing.

All of the men in Israel should have been gone out to battle. The woman was in her right to bathe, not knowing any man was left in the city.

When we are out of the will and timing of God, our mind is not on the things of heaven. David's own desire consumed him and he became obsessed to conquer that woman.

Because of his intense pride at that time, it no longer mattered to David what was right or wrong. It no longer mattered that she was another man's wife. Due to pride searing his conscience from desire, it didn't even matter that the woman's husband was one of his most faithful servants.

All that mattered to David was that his desire be fulfilled, at any cost.

It is sad to say that when a person comes to this point, they are usually capable of any and all sin. I have seen friends and ministers fall to the pride of uncontrolled desire, and some lose everything they have given their whole lives for.

In verses 4 and 5, David sent for the woman and slept with her — and she conceived.

Instead of waking up and repenting, David went deeper into sin to cover his pride, his own ways. He turned into another man, one totally opposite of the character that God had exalted in him. He began to plot, scheme and lie to cover his error. He began to betray his people and his household by pretending to be something he wasn't.

When uncontrolled desire consumes a person, normalcy leaves. It almost seems as if common sense is nowhere to be found. Extreme behavior patterns surface, because the desire has become so great that the sense of right and wrong has been numbed.

The people who have gone to this stage of desire will cut off association with all those around them who have a different standard. They will gather others to themselves to support their ways, some twisting scripture and principles to do it. Uncontrolled desire has blinded them from the timing and relationships of God.

Missing God's timing through desire causes a person to devour anything that stands in the way. When we step out of the correct timing, it means we step into every vice that can accompany the wrong. When uncontrolled desire leads a life without repentance, then acts of betrayal, lying, stealing, cheating, lust, and eventually physical death will follow.

From verses 6 through 24, you can read how David attempted to deceive and flatter Uriah, the woman's husband, to go home and sleep with his wife so it would appear the baby was his. But Uriah was so faithful and trusting of David's kindness, he vowed even deeper loyalty to his country and refused to go home to his wife.

Out of desperation, with no sense of right or wrong, David had Uriah sent to the front of the battle and killed.

Loving Comfort

Another area of pride David had to face in his heart, that caused him to miss the timing of God, was that he was *too comfortable.*

David was surrounded by people who said "yes" to whatever he dictated. Because his heart had become turned by comfort, he used those that God had sent to him, for his own gain and protection.

If you are not surrounded by those who can sharpen you like iron, you are being set up for a great fall. Many friends and ministers I have seen pad themselves inside a group of "yes men." They surround themselves with these people, because it comforts them. The problem is, when these ministers and friends surely fall, those on the cutting edge cannot hear their cry for help because the "padding" is so thick from those they are surrounded by. You cannot stay accurate when you surround yourself with unreality.

Loving comfort will rob us from hitting the timings of God. When we are too comfortable, we will lose our cutting edge.

If we run from confrontation because we are afraid it might shake our comfort and the "little fort" we've built, then we are heading straight into defeat.

Comfort zones will not always throw someone into sexual sins. They are the people who usually fall prey to religious sin and can be led by religious spirits. They are the ones who are easily offended.

A minister once said to me, "Well, Roberts, I feel that all we need to do is just preach the gospel."

Well, I believe that, too.

But there is more to the full gospel than just giving it out. There is an accuracy in timing we must learn to hit, and one of the items on our checklist helping us learn it, is in these character safeguards.

Many who like comfort zones will not like this book. Learning to walk with God's timing means responsibility and an amount of pressure, and comfort-people have put aside both of those.

How does a person end up loving comfort more than God? There are several reasons.

One is sin in their heart. First John 2:16 says:

> For all that is in the world, the lust of the flesh, and the lust of the eyes, and the pride of life, is not of the Father, but is of the world.

The Amplified Version of the same verse says, the **assurance in one's own resources or in the stability of earthly things** will cause a person to love comfort more than the Father.

Another reason is that they liked a certain move of God and came into an understanding of it, so they are more comfortable with a maintenance ministry than moving with what God is doing today.

Sometimes breaking new ground, going where people have not gone in ways that seem untraditional, can get you into trouble with your peers. Some are afraid that being different than other churches would hurt their church growth.

There are certain areas we would all like to stay in. I have my favorites, too. But like it or not, times and seasons all come to an end and new ones always begin. If you get caught in the wrong time because of comfort, captivity and sin will begin to settle in with you.

When we read the stories of the men who did great exploits in the Bible, we can see by their lives they certainly did not seek comfort or security, nor did they live in comfortable, stable and secure times. If you begin to sense a different way than you have been used to seeing, accept it. Do not reject the calling or hold it away from you. On the other hand, test every spirit. It is not smart to go to the extreme and think, "Well, this is a different thing, so it must be from God!"

Some of you reading this book are trying to make your life fit the way you have it planned. But, to move accurately in the timing of God, we have to be willing to have some plans turned upside down from the way we originally thought.

Although I am a young adult, the Lord has taught me something very important that has kept me out of the comfort zone. Years ago, He said, "Do not try to live your life according to what other people do." I have learned to live my life two ways: one, according to the timing of God; and two, according to the calling upon my life.

On the other hand, allowing people to think you are special because of doing things God's way is also a trap of the devil to hinder you. Because I did go in God's timing and live my life differently than many others my age, people called me unique. I did not know how to respond to that, so I would agree that I was different.

Then the Lord said to me, "You quit agreeing with a lie! You are NOT a unique case. That will open a door of pride to you if you keep saying that. Because you are walking in My time, what is happening in your life is normal. It is not unique nor peculiar, nor an oddity. Your life is normal."

The people who obey God are normal. The people who walk in God's timing are normal. Those who do not know spiritual time and walk in the ways of the earth are the ones who are different. They are out of step with God's way.

Other people used to tell me I was strange, and I would say, "Yes, I know, but I'm not changing." After the Lord began to talk to me about that too, I had to stop saying that. I began to say, "No, I'm not weird, I'm normal. I just know how to walk in God's timing for my life."

Christians who are single particularly need to look for God's timing in connection with marriage. Comfort, loneliness and security can be great pitfalls in which to miss the timing of God. Even if you know the one, there is a correct timing. The Holy Spirit said, "There are going to be many people in this day who will come close to aborting their callings because of trying to make things happen in the area of marriage."

Do not allow people or circumstances to put you in a box or place you in a certain slot and keep you there. Have faith that God knows what He is doing, and keep your mind under control. Do not allow your mind to abort you from the time that God has placed you in.

Loving comfort puts us in danger of captivity, coming against a move of God, coming against the Word of the Lord and coming against the brethren that might not believe exactly like we do.

A Heart for the People

The third character flaw David had in 2 Samuel, was *his lack of heart for his people.*

> **Then David said unto the messenger, Thus shalt thou say unto Joab, [concerning the planned death of Uriah] Let not this thing displease thee, for the sword devoureth one as well as another: make thy battle more**

strong against the city, and overthrow it: and encourage thou him.

2 Samuel 11:25

When we have a heart for the people, as believers and leaders alike, we will listen to heaven and be by their side, through good times and bad. David sent the people out to face the times alone, because he felt superior to them at that time; but as he stayed behind, he fell into sin.

One of the saddest sights in the earth is a minister who has lost his heart for the people. When a person loses his heart for the human race and turns that desire towards himself, sin will devastate him.

Throughout the Old Testament, God showed Himself strong on behalf of the prophets whose hearts were turned towards the people.

Although the prophets were appalled at the sin of the people, they would rend their own garments and cry out for repentance with them, as if they had sinned themselves.

Jonah was a prophet who had a difficult time learning compassion for the people. God taught him a hard lesson, and we never hear about him again.

Moses constantly considered the people over himself. Even with the great tasks he had to face, only once did he turn his heart against the people, reacting in anger and accusation. He disobeyed God in it, spoke what he felt and called the people some accurate names! But from that one, serious mistake, he was not allowed to enter the Promised Land (Num. 20). God takes the people and the representation of His heart towards them very seriously.

Gideon was a leader who had a heart for the people. Judges chapter 6, verse 12 says:

> And the angel of the Lord appeared unto him, and said unto him, The Lord is with thee, thou mighty man of valour.

Where would your heart be if the angel of the Lord appeared to you and told you that the Lord was with you? Look at Gideon's heart:

> And Gideon said unto him, Oh my Lord, if the Lord be with *us*, why then is all this befallen *us*? and where be all his miracles which our fathers told us . . . ?

> Verse 13

Gideon did not single himself out from the people. He did not stick out his chest, puff himself up and say, "I have got it. I have arrived. Yes, I am chosen, God is with *me*. Stick with *me* and you will make it." No, he answered with his heart, and it showed where it was. He had a heart for the people.

In verse 14, the Lord said something very significant to him.

> And the Lord looked upon him, and said, GO IN THIS THY MIGHT, and thou shalt save Israel from the hand of the Midianites . . .

What was the might of Gideon that the Lord was referring to? His heart for the people and his heart for miracles. The two ingredients added together produce a sensitivity to the correct timings of God.

The Lord went on to tell him in verse 16, that Gideon and the people would smite the enemy "as one man."

When leadership and believers have a heart for one another, a unity comes that cannot be penetrated by the work of darkness. The Body of Christ, when unified in heart, is invincible.

Of course, there are many verses that show the heart of Jesus while He walked on the earth. But one in particular expresses how timing and a heart for the people walk hand in hand. According to John chapter 13, verse 1, Jesus knew the timing had come to leave this world. But a very significant part of that verse states, ". . . having loved his own . . . he loved them unto the end."

Although He was betrayed by those closest to Him, persecuted, misrepresented, lied about and beaten, His heart remained fixed for the benefit of all mankind, to His death. As a result, He triumphantly fulfilled the plan of the Father for all eternity.

Whatever God has called you to do, be it to lead or to follow, do it with a heart for the people.

5

Blessings of the Right Timing

The most important thing in all these days is to find the correct timing of God in your life, and to walk with it.

One of the most successful stories in the Bible concerning two people who operated in the correct timing of God, was Esther and Mordecai. Esther's name means "star",[1] and as far as I am concerned, she gets one in my book.

Just as we have discussed character flaws that cause one to miss the timing, we need to discuss some attributes that cause us to come into the right timing.

Godly Authority

In the Book of Esther, in the Old Testament, an interesting story unfolds. King Ahasuerus has just alleviated Queen Vashti of her royal duties, and the call for a new queen was proclaimed throughout the region.

Mordecai's uncle had died and left a daughter, Esther, whom he had taken in and raised as his own. Esther became one of the many women taken into the palace to stand before the king.

---

[1]Strong's Concordance, "ECTER," Hebrew Dictionary, reference #635 persian der., KJV Open Bible. *Hebrew - Myrtle - (Intercessor)*

Although she was on her own in the palace, Mordecai asked that she not reveal her kindred nor show that she was a Jew. Keeping this secret was not deceptive; it was not the time to reveal it and Mordecai sensed it. His wisdom caused him to be exalted later on. Because she chose to submit to his authority in her life and listen to his godly advice, it caused her to enter into God's correct timing, and it saved the entire Jewish nation from destruction. (Esth. 2:10,20.)

There are many good books on spiritual authority. Godly authority is designed by God for our protection and covering. Finding and submitting to godly authority creates a strength inside of us and gives us the added courage to walk in obedience. It is ordained by God and not appointed by a friend or an idea.

In the Book of Numbers, chapter 16, Korah and those most popular in the camp, took on the fatal assumption that they were in as much authority over the people as Moses and Aaron. They voiced the same murmur we still hear today from those who know no better, "We are just as holy as you and we can hear God for ourselves. Who do you think you are trying to be the leader?" (v. 3.)

It is true that every New Testament believer has the unction within and has the ability to hear from God for themselves concerning themselves. But all believers are not the same in one sense — God has ordained for some to be endowed in the five-fold ministry, a ministry of leadership and training for the Body of Christ (Eph. 4:11-16.) He gave them titles — Apostle, Prophet, Evangelist, Pastor, and Teacher. Their function is to mature the saints and teach them how to hear God for themselves, so they will not be deceived. These are gifts given by Jesus and the responsibility and pressure that accompany them can be staggering at times. Most of those called into the five-fold ministry have never sought those gifts.

The Apostle Paul goes on to write in verses 17 and 18 that once we understand the function of the five-fold, then we should:

> **walk not as other Gentiles** [or carnal ones] **walk, in the vanity** [emptiness] **of their mind, Having the understanding darkened, being alienated from the life of God through the ignorance that is in them, because of the blindness of their heart.**

Do you see what Paul is saying? If we walk in our own ways, as one not under authority, we will not know the timing of God for our lives because we will be surrounded by darkness and blindness. Being "alienated from the life of God" for the believer means to not walk according to His time and season. There is abundant life when we are walking with God. As a matter of fact, you cannot walk with God and be out of His timing.

We do not put leadership up on a pedestal, but we respect and honor them for teaching us and giving their lives for the ways of the Lord. By doing so and learning from their lives and ministries, it causes our hearts to be sensitive to the correct seasons of God. As a result, maturity and blessings follow us.

It is imperative that we submit ourselves to godly authority in this hour, believer and leader alike, so that the Spirit of the Lord can accomplish His endtime plan through us and save the nations of today.

Motives Must Be Right

After Esther was chosen to be a maiden in the palace, it was time for her to be brought before the king. The palace had a set regulation, that whatever the maiden asked for or desired, was to be given to her. (Esth. 2:13.)

Such a vast ruling would certainly expose the greed or lack of it in a person's heart! The remaining maidens must have asked for much, for in verse 15 it says:

> **Now when the turn of Esther** [came]. . . **she required nothing but what Hegai the king's chamberlain, the keeper of the women, appointed.**

Here is the result of a right motive:

> **And Esther obtained favor in the sight of all them that looked upon her.**

To obtain the favor of God for the nations, we must have the right motives in our heart. Many people have attempted to cover their motives through flattery or deception, but the truth is always revealed. In this hour, time is speeding up because the end is drawing near. That means the works of men are revealed in a quicker way, good and bad. The right motive, even when you make a mistake, will protect you and keep you sensitive to the heart of God.

To those who are called of God and anointed, there is a special need to be careful of motives.

Some time ago, I was in a meeting with pastors and teachers, and at lunch, they were talking about "how everyone thinks they are prophets today." Finally, they asked me what I thought.

I got bold and said, "Your motives are not right. The only reason one would be so touchy about prophets is if they are nervous for their own ministries and pastorates.

"If you talk about something happening in the Church in the right spirit, there is no criticism. You can be cautious, but you will not be judgmental nor coming against something God is doing or against some other person in the Body. That kind of discussion with the right motive is led by the Holy Spirit. It brings truth and an earnest seeking of God's help.

"There is something wrong with the way you are talking about prophets and the restoration of that office. Remember the healing revival? Remember how many people misused the gifts? Remember the extremes that came — no doctors, no medicine and so forth?

"Why didn't you throw out all the healing when those errors and false manifestations began to occur?

"What about the faith movement and all of those on the fringes who got into presumption? Why didn't you throw out the faith message?

"What about prosperity and all those who misunderstood and gave money thinking they would get a new car or a new house? Why didn't you throw out prosperity?

"You didn't do that because there was still truth in the middle of error. There was a pure message from God, a revelation, in there somewhere. Well, right now God is restoring deliverance, interession and the prophetic. Yes, some imbalance is going to be involved. But are you going to throw out the pureness of God's truth along with the flesh and the demonic that try to

51

get involved? Are you going to throw the baby out with the bath water?"

I hope they really heard what the Holy Spirit was saying, or those people will miss God's timing and season for today because of wrong motives in their hearts.

Your motives must not only be right in ministry, but also in studying and talking about the ministry entrusted to others. Pray for those in error; but they are God's servants to straighten out, not yours.

Esther's motive was not to take and heap riches upon herself. Her motive was just to be obedient and to respect the king and his palace. As a result, the king favored her above all the women and placed the crown of a queen upon her head. (Verse 17.) Because Esther displayed a humble and correct motive, the favor she received exalted her to a place of position and authority. Her strong character allowed God to have her strategically in place when the enemy attempted to destroy the Jewish people. Esther was in her place for the correct time.

Fasting and Prayer

Prayer is the power source to a spirit-filled life. I will not attempt to cover all the benefits of prayer in this book, but I do want to bring out how fasting and prayer prepared Esther to accomplish her task.

Prayer is the vehicle of travel in the spirit. The steering wheel is the Word of God and the fuel is your persistence. There is no wall too thick that prayer cannot plow through. Prayer is vital to our spiritual strength.

In chapters 3 and 4 of the Book of Esther, King Ahasuerus had promoted the wicked Haman over all the princes of the region. Haman had a pride problem, and he did not like it that Mordecai refused to bow down to him. Once he discovered that Mordecai was a Jew, he decided to destroy the entire Jewish nation. The king unknowingly granted his consent, and the decree was published throughout the region.

Mordecai sent word to Esther, telling her to make known to the king of her Jewish nationality. Esther replied that she had not been called for by the king in thirty days, and anyone who entered the inner court of the palace would be put to death unless the king raised the golden sceptre.

Mordecai responded:

> . . . **who knoweth whether thou art come to the kingdom for such a time as this?**
>
> **Esther 4:14**

God will cause a particular message to rise at a specific time. There will always be certain people who will rise at a certain time to do a certain work. Just as Esther was appointed to arise for one job, so will many be called upon today.

Strong character and a strong spirit will position you to know exactly what you are to do and where you are to go, and nothing more or nothing less.

Gideon was a man who had just one job. In Judges, chapter 8, verse 23, the people pleaded with him to rule over them and be their king, because of his success. But Gideon knew his place, his position and the season of God. He answered, **"I will not rule over you, neither shall my son rule over you: the Lord**

shall rule over you" (v. 23). Gideon's job was to bring deliverance and help, and he fulfilled it.

Ecclesiastes, chapter 3, verse 1 says:

> **To every thing there is a season, and a time to every purpose under the heaven.**

There is a correct season and a correct time to come forth and do the job you are being positioned to do. Prayer and fasting will keep you alert to God's plan.

From Mordecai's exhortation, Esther rose up in her spirit and moved to accept her position for the hour. She instructed Mordecai and all of the Jews with him to fast and pray for three days, no food or water. She and her maidens vowed to do the same. (Esth. 4:16.)

To experience the realms of God, we must be adventurous in prayer. I am sure that Esther and the Jewish nation ventured out in a high level of prayer to receive the understanding that came. Esther, during those three days, received the detailed instructions on how to win the favor of the king for the Jewish nation.

The story goes on, after the three days of prayer and fasting, that Esther invited the king and Haman to dinner. The king graciously accepted and begged her to tell him what she desired of him. Instead of blurting out all she knew, she had built discipline through her godly character and her prayer and fasting. She knew what she was to do. She invited the king and Haman back the second night.

When they returned, the king's heart was ready to hear all that his queen would ask of him. She explained the dilemma and revealed that Haman had plotted the destruction of the Jews.

Because of her courage and timing, not only was Haman hung on the gallows he had prepared for Mordecai, but so were all of his sons, and Mordecai was exalted second only to the king.

In her strength, Esther went all the way. She not only rid her people of the main enemy through Haman, but she executed his ten sons as well. (Esth. 9:13).

That is the anointing of those who walk in the timing of God. They will not stop at the first phase of victory — they pursue until the entire problem is conquered.

But the story does not end there. Being accurate in the timing of God produces a harvest of souls. After the victory was proclaimed throughout the region, conviction came to the people.

> **And many of the people of the land became Jews;**
> **for the fear of the Jews fell upon them.**
>
> **Esther 8:17**

To this day, the Jewish people celebrate the victory God granted their nation through Esther and Mordecai.

Walking in the correct timing of God produces total victory in every area. The sick are healed, the oppressed go free, the lost are saved — the enemy is defeated and the Kingdom of God progresses!

First Chronicles, chapter 12, verse 32 states:

> **And of the children of Issachar, which were men**
> **that had understanding of the times, to know what**
> **Israel ought to do . . ..**

In Strong's Concordance, the word "understanding" in the Hebrew means "to perceive."[2] It is

---

[2]Strong's Concordance, "understanding," reference #995 and 998.

the will of God that we perceive by our spirits the time we are in, and then to know the job we are to do within that timing.

6

Receiving Remedy and Restoration

How do you know what God is saying? How can you be sure to be in the correct timing of God?

By applying the spiritual principles covered in this book, you can set your heart to hear from God and be in the right place at the right time.

Let me give you some points on how to tell God's time:

• **Do not seek another person's opinion as absolute direction on what you sense in your spirit.** Go to the Father in prayer and say, "Father, show me the timing of these things. Help my perception to be stronger."

• **Believe what you get in your spirit.** What you hear in your head is probably wrong.

• **Seek God on the message you hear or read from ministers of the Gospel.** A few years ago, I began to feel the anointing for warfare surfacing again in the Body of Christ, and I wrote a book, *The Invading Force.*[1]

Many people said, "Boy, he's full of youthful zeal and fire. He is so full of zeal." Every time I heard that, my stomach would turn. I knew the message was a word from God delivered in His timing. I knew the

---

[1]*The Invading Force,* Tulsa: Harrison House, 1987.

attitudes of those people were a sign of spiritual complacency. God's message was being patronized by them, not received.

If that message was "youthful zeal," then I want it when I am 80, if the Lord tarries that long.

But I heard that so often, I began to check myself. I went back to the Lord and prayed, "God, tell me what time it is. Am I preaching what You are doing? Is this a time of war that we are coming into?"

At that time, everyone wanted to hear about love and prosperity and nice things.

Down in my spirit, God kept saying to me, "A time of conflict, a time of war has the Church come into. This is not a time of peace but a time of spiritual conflict. You need this anointing for this time."

I realized that warfare is always a precedence for spiritual harvest, and it was settled forever.

One of the easiest ways to check a message or a word is to pray and ask God, then stay with what you hear in your spirit.

• **Listen to the prophecies you hear.** When those things begin to be fulfilled, you know God's timing is changing.

The Lord said to me once, "When events (such as the walls coming down in Eastern Europe) take place in the last days, they are not to be analyzed but taken advantage of. My Church needs to quit looking and analyzing everything but see the door that has been opened and go through it."

The events over the past year in Europe and Asia have shown that God will open the windows and doors for the Church to reap the harvest before the end comes. Look for the doors of opportunity to preach the Gospel of the Kingdom.

The Church of the last days is to be a Church that works. The Church will not have time to write books on endtime prophecy. They will be too busy fulfilling those endtime prophecies! We have a duty to "do," not a show to watch. God's clock says to me that revival is in progress and something is about to break open worldwide.

What if You Miss it?

Suppose you do miss the due season. What if, for some reason, you miss the entire timing of something? God can redeem the time.

> **See then that ye walk circumspectly, not as fools, but as wise,**
>
> **Redeeming the time, because the days are evil.**
>
> **Ephesians 5:15,16**

Redeeming the time means "rescue from loss"[2] God can recover and redeem the time through His grace and mercy. If you miss it, get up, repent, find out what you did wrong, and go on. Use your mistakes as stepping stones, not stumbling blocks.

In these last days, we have come so close to the end, it seems there may be some things that cannot be recovered. But I also believe in miracles. God will do what He can in the time that is left.

How do you get to the place where God will redeem the time?

---

[2]Strong's Concordance, "redeeming," reference 1805.

You pray in repentance something like this, "Father, I'm sorry for missing it. If You arrange the time for me to do it again, I'll do it Your way. Forgive me for making the mistake. Thank You for redeeming the time for me."

Some of you may be saying, "I was middle-aged or old when I got born again. I have quit running and agreed to do what God called me to do."

Ask God to redeem the time for you so that you can do more in the latter part of your life than you did in the beginning.

I pray this book will help each reader to better discern the times. I encourage you to seek God about the seasons going on in your life, your church, your nation and world. I believe that many will hear from God and the separation of the wheat and the tares will find them among the wheat.

A Prophecy Concerning Prophets

[Editor's Note: This is a word given by Roberts Liardon in an international meeting in Sweden, March, 1990.]

The Word of the Lord comes unto me, saying, "The prophet's office has a responsibility to declare the times and seasons that I have decided for the earth, to teach men to walk accurately in them. For in the day in which you live," says the Spirit of the Lord, "it is crucial that men have a greater revelation of the times and seasons. The prophet's ministry will have a great role in teaching and in demonstrating, for there are demonstrations of time," says the Spirit of God, "that will come about in this day.

"So don't be scared or nervous over the words that will be brought pertaining to the time in which you live and the seasons into which you have come. The prophet's ministry has a calling on it that is like no other day, for people run everywhere, seeking to have an understanding of what is happening and what shall be. Why do the nations move as they do? Why do men act as they do? There is a reason," says the Spirit of God.

"Time has come close to (Nations and men), and they know not how to read. They do not know how to read that which is written before them. They do not know how to see what time it is according to God's clock. They run searching and asking, 'What shall be? What shall be'?

"And I have designed that My prophets shall carry My time and declare it not just to My people but to those around My people. For there already have come false prophets in the earth who have begun to declare time, but they are wrong. They have their time, and it is false. And it is easy for secular man, for a man who knows not My Spirit to believe what they say. The words (of the false prophets) sound so good, and men do not want to hear what My prophets have to say because (My prophets) do not declare peace. They do not declare the prosperity (prosperous times) that men wish to hear, nor do they declare the safety that attracts men. But My prophets declare My path and My season, according to a higher law of greater strengths.

"And the man of the earth recoils against a higher law. But My prophets shall speak and declare, and they shall demonstrate things pertaining to time. There will come battles between the true and the false, and whose word will stand?

"They will say to My prophets, 'My word shall stand because I spoke of this and this, and it has occurred.'

"But I will cause My prophets to speak a more indepth word, a more intelligent word, because false prophets speak very generally (in very general terms). There is coming a fine tuning and a more intelligent word through My prophets that will astound the governments of the world, for (My prophets) will know their secrets and the times those secrets were made. They will make those things known, and then the people of the world will become aware also of My time," says the Lord.

"Yes, there are some words that you hold in your heart. Some have held them for many seasons," says the Lord. "And you've asked yourself many times, 'When is this word inside of me going to come forth?' Sometimes you thought it would be at this moment for a certain people, but the word did not come forth. There were some who tried to give forth the words through human efforts, but they did not come with the force they were designed to come with."

And the Spirit of the Lord says, "The words that some of you have held for many seasons — you have come now to the season when those words will begin to come out of your mouth. And they will come with unction, not just things stated according to natural ways, but they will come with great unction, with a force that has not been known before.

"So you have not missed my time, and that which you've held in your spirit has not been wrong. You have just waited for the time. For the word of the Lord shall now have a new door. A new door of utterance shall be given to the prophet's ministry, a new door for the prophetic gift. A new understanding has now come unto the people who desired and prayed to have an understanding. And because they have desired," says the Lord, "That has helped open up the door of utterance for the ministry of the prophet. The word of the Lord has a new door to come through, with more force and more intelligence," says the Lord.

To contact Roberts Liardon
write:

Roberts Liardon Ministries
P. O. Box 23238
Minneapolis, MN 55423

*Please include your prayer requests
and comments when you write.*